THE TECHNIQUE OF VIOLIN PLAYING

THE JOACHIM METHOD

THE TECHNIQUE OF VIOLIN PLAYING

THE JOACHIM METHOD

KARL COURVOISIER

DOVER PUBLICATIONS, INC.
Mineola, New York

Bibliographical Note

This Dover edition, first published in 2006, is an unabridged republication of *The Technics of Violin Playing,* originally published by G. Schirmer, Inc., New York, in 1897. H. E. Krehbiel was the editor and translator of the English version. The "Table of Contents," which appeared at the end of the original edition, has been moved to page 1.

International Standard Book Number: 0-486-45274-3

Manufactured in the United States of America
Dover Publications, Inc., 31 East 2nd Street, Mineola, N.Y. 11501

SECOND REVISED EDITION.

THE

TECHNICS OF VIOLIN PLAYING,

BY

KARL COURVOISIER,

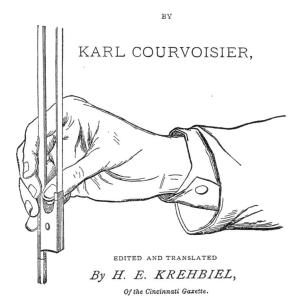

EDITED AND TRANSLATED

By H. E. KREHBIEL,

Of the Cincinnati Gazette.

NEW YORK:

G. SCHIRMER.

1897.

[Original title page]

TO THE

MUSICAL CLUB

OF

CINCINNATI.

TABLE OF CONTENTS.

PREFACE.

I BELIEVE this little work needs no apology. There is justification for its appearance in the fact that it is a succinct and, I hope, clear exposition of the essential features of the system of technical violin instruction pursued by Joseph Joachim, the greatest living violinist and teacher. The author, Herr Karl Courvoisier, of Frankfort-on-the-Main, himself a teacher of wide experience, is a pupil of Herr Joachim, from whom he received a public testimonial for the fidelity and skill with which his teachings had been grasped and utilized. In 1873 Herr Courvoisier published a brochure of 43 pages which he called "Die Grundlage der Violin-Technik." Its manuscript had previously been submitted to Herr Joachim, who honored it and its author with a letter, of which the following is a translation :

"MY DEAR COURVOISIER :—The query whether you ought to publish your treatise on violin playing, which I return herewith, I can only answer with an unqualified yes. I have read it carefully and am rejoiced to learn from it how faithfully you have heeded my instructions, how firmly you are grounded on my teachings, and how skillfully you apply the results of your own experience as teacher. It is my opinion that your book will offer material aid to all violin players who are earnestly striving to acquire a technique which will enable them to present the musical idea freed from the slack of one-sided fiddler habits. It will, therefore, be nothing else than a pleasure to me if you make use of my favorable opinion of your MS. in applying to a publisher. My best wishes go with it into publicity.

"With sincere respect,
"JOSEPH JOACHIM."

In 1878 Herr Courvoisier published a second work on the same subject ("Die Violin-Technik. Cöln, in Commission bei Pet. Jos. Tonger, Hof 33.") In this, instead of contenting himself with a revision of his "Grundlage, &c.," he widened the scope of his inquiry so as to comprehend the whole field of violin technics. These two works are the base of the present brochure, in which my work of editing and translating has been governed by the purpose to present all the vital features of Herr Courvoisier's second book in the convenient form of a small pamphlet, and in a style suited to the needs of violin players, teachers, and pupils alike.

In the form of an appendix, I have added, with the assistance of Mr. J. A. Broekhoven, a studious and experienced musician, a list of the best published exercises and studies for the violin, carefully graduated from elementary to the most advanced degree, for the guidance of teachers.

It is because of the great importance of the subject treated, and the weight of the authority which it bears, that I bespeak for it a kind reception from the musicians of the United States. H. E. K.

CINCINNATI, April, 1880.

INTRODUCTION.

THE most difficult musical instruments to play are those of the viol tribe. The reason of this is found in the fact that their manipulation requires widely different functions from the hands of the performer. Their marvelous capacity for eloquent and varied expression, however, compensates for the vast study and practice necessary for the acquirement of proficiency on them.

The functions of the hands in violin playing are these:

The fingers of the left hand form the tones by varying the length of the vibrating segments of the strings by pressing them against the finger-board at fixed points.

The right hand causes the strings to sound by drawing the bow across them; it also determines the dynamic gradations of the tones (loud or soft, and the intermediate nuances), and the style of their succession (slurred or detached).

Both hands co-operate to control the infinite variety in the rhythmical order of the tones.

From this general explanation we deduce at once the most important law of violin playing, viz:

THE PRESSURE OF THE FINGER UPON THE STRING MUST

EXCEED THAT OF THE BOW; otherwise the vibrations caused by the moving bow, which ought to be checked at the point touched by the finger, will be continued beyond, and the tone will be indistinct, lower in pitch, if not destroyed.

In order that the fingers of the left hand may attain the requisite strength and at the same time the greatest possible freedom in movement, their position must be prepared, in the manner to be described, by the position of the body, the arm, and the hand.

PART I.

THE LEFT SIDE.—TONE FORMATION.

SECTION I.

ATTITUDE OF THE BODY.—POSITION OF THE VIOLIN.

THE player should stand erect, with the weight of his body resting on his left foot; his right foot should rest upon the floor, a little forward and to the right, and at a slight angle to the left foot. This position secures solidity and repose for the left side, upon which the violin rests, and the freedom for the right which is requisite for the proper handling of the bow. There should be no laxity in the muscles of the upper half of the body; the chest should be thrown out, to allow freedom in respiration, and the head should be kept upright, leaning, if at all, to the left, over the violin, rather than to the right. This position of the head, besides being the most graceful, renders the reading of the notes easier than any other.

The broad end of the violin should be placed well up on the left collar-bone and be held in the proper position, as firm as possible, by pressure from the left side of the jaw—not the chin—which should rest upon the belly of the instrument, to the left of the tail-piece. The position of the violin should be :—

7

1. Such that the strings will run horizontally from the bridge to the nut; the scroll or head must be in a line with the chin;

2. Not straight out, (that is, not at right angles with a straight line drawn across the shoulders,) but with a decided tendency to the left; the deflection, however, should not be so great that the right hand can not draw the bow from nut to point at right angles with the strings;

3. With its right side tilted downward so 'far as to enable the right arm in executing a stroke on the first string (*E*) to escape brushing against the body. This tilt is at an angle of nearly forty-five degrees, that is, about midway between a perpendicular and a horizontal position of the violin.

These directions have it for their general purpose to render easy the position and movements of the left arm, and the fingers of the left hand. The first has an additional purpose, viz: to keep the bow from slipping to the side of its point of contact with the strings, by enabling it to move across a level instead of an incline; the third obviates the raising the right arm to an unnecessary height in playing, particularly on the *G*-string. Excellent aids to a good and firm position for the violin, especially in case of an illy-adapted shoulder, neck, or jaw, is the use of a violin-holder, or chin-rest, and a small cushion or roll of cloth placed under the coat or vest between the violin and collar-bone. The chin-rest is an oval plate of ebony, slightly hollowed on its upper surface to receive the curve of the jaw, fastened to the edge of the violin to the left of the tail-piece, extending over but not touching the belly.

These aids are useful even to a player with high shoulders, short neck, and broad jaw; for the hand has so much to do that it must be prohibited from participating in the simple holding of the instrument. To permit it to do this would be to waste a certain amount of useful power, to hamper its movements along the neck, on which it must be left free and ready to occupy any position with ease and certainty at the will of the player; moreover, to grasp the neck with the hand would shake or change the position of the violin when it became necessary to shift the hand, and the purity of intonation would be endangered. When the player wishes to rest his head and shoulder from the strain imposed in holding the violin, he should take time either during rests in the music or passages which do not require changes in the position of the left hand. The use of the chin-rest and cushion obviates the need of raising the left shoulder, which is very tiresome.

SECTION II.

POSITIONS OF THE ARM AND HAND.

The left hand should not grasp the neck of the violin, but should be extended, with the palm turned toward the player, and the neck coming between the thumb and forefinger should touch lightly against the thumb. The principal purpose in closing the forefinger upon it is to fix the points of intonation, that is to say, to bring the bases of the forefingers into a position from which the movement to bring the tips into contact with the strings at the proper distances can best be executed; to guard the neck from slipping along the thumb is only a secondary purpose.

We find in all the published "Violin Schools" and "Methods" a normal position prescribed for the left hand and arm, viz: that compelled by grasping the following chord:

The distance that the hand is raised above the finger-board to enable the four fingers to stop the four strings to produce these notes, and the distance that the elbow is compelled from the breast is described as the proper position for all cases.

This view is incorrect.

In the first place, a player never begins with, and indeed seldom plays, music in four parts, except in single chords; the violin is chiefly a melody instrument, that is, it is principally used homophonically. Besides, with the hand in this position, it is impossible to bring the fingers down so as to exert a perpendicular pressure upon the *E*-string; they will all touch it at an angle and force it toward the edge of the finger-board. In quadruple, and even triple, stops, the fingers that control the *E*-string (with the exception of the little finger) would be in a very peculiar situation, and one very far from that which is proper and necessary in homophonic playing upon this string. Instead, therefore, of prescribing a coercive measure, which will only prove a torture to the beginner and an inconvenience to the schooled player, it would have been wiser to have looked for a governing principle plainer to the comprehension of the beginner.

The matter is not difficult of regulation. One-part playing upon a single string is amenable to the requirement already suggested, viz: the finger tips must rest perpendicularly on the strings, not only in order that they may exert a sufficiently powerful pressure, but also that no neighboring string be touched. This latter purpose has the weight of a rule, for the reason that it must be possible at any time to connect the tone of one string with that of another by a slur, or to sound the two together. If the base of the forefinger lies any considerable distance under the neck of the violin or below the finger-board, the tip of this finger can not be brought down perpendicularly upon the string, much less the tips of the other fingers. Moreover, if the base of the forefinger is too far from the point which its tip is to touch, the other fingers will hardly be able to reach their proper places, and it will be impossible to bring the left side of the hand toward the neck without twisting the forefinger, and if this is once disturbed it will not be able to resume its position of its own strength. On the other hand, by approaching the base of the forefinger to the point opposite the resting place of its tip (to do which will require a sharp bend of the finger), not only are the other fingers assisted to their places lengthwise of the string, but the side of the hand is involuntarily turned toward the neck, and a special injunction to this end is not needed; instead, nothing more than a caution against laxity.

The simple rule is this:

Place the tip of the forefinger perpendicularly upon the proper place on the string, and draw the base of the finger as near it as possible.

This rule, which will enable every fully developed hand to apply its fingers firmly and cleanly, is an infallible one, not only for one string, but for every other one, for every position and for the entire technique of the left hand.

In the sense claimed in these methods there is, therefore, no normal position; instead we are justified in assuming four equally correct positions for the hand and arm. The lowest, which controls the *E*-string, permits only two-thirds of the forefinger to be seen above the edge of the finger-board, while for the highest, which controls the *G*-string, the base of the forefinger is raised to the level or above the edge of the finger-board, according to the length of the finger. In this position the elbow must be thrust out so far in front of the breast as to lie directly under the declining right rim of of the violin, while in the first it can occupy a more comfortable position, say under the left rim of the instrument.

Practice will show, however, that this distinction of four positions is not an urgent necessity, but that the arm and hand can find a position from which two neighboring strings can be governed, a change being compelled only by a transfer of fingers to a third string. Instead, therefore, of fixing a number of normal positions for the hand and arm, I would advise that the extreme limits described in the preceding paragraph be kept in mind, and that, within them, the hand and arm be moved without restraint around the neck of the violin as required by the service they owe the fingers. They are the slaves of the fingers, and are not to be permitted to hold any arbitrary position or to change one once taken, except at the bidding of the fingers, which alone determine time and distances of movements for the purposes of intonation.

Other essential features in the regulation of the hand and arm are : a. *Complete laxity of the elbow joint;* b. *Repose, but firmness, of the wrist-joint.*

SECTION III.

POSITIONS AND FUNCTIONS OF THE THUMB.

The province of the thumb is to resist the pressure exerted by the fingers; it will, of course, feel the pressure, but it must not participate in it. As a rule, it is best that the neck of the violin should lean against the lower joint of the thumb, as this affords a more solid support; and the tip is left freer for action; it should not come in contact with the loose skin between the thumb and forefinger, however, for two reasons: first, this would lift the fingers too high above the finger-board; second, the skin, by clinging to the neck, would be apt to embarrass the movement of the hand in shifting its position, and effect the correctness of the estimate as to the distance moved.

In the first three positions the location of the thumb is governed by that of the forefinger, and is, consequently, variable. As a rule, its best position is somewhat forward of the base of the forefinger, and in any case, a little in front of

Fig. I. A front view of the entire position. Note the turn of the violin to the left, the downward tilt of its right rim, and the horizontal direction of the strings. The left elbow is thrust in front of the breast as required to enable the fingers to govern the tones in the first position on the *G*-string (a, b, c, d). Two positions of the right arm are drawn, showing the limits of its elevation and depression, as when playing on the outside strings.

the tip. In this position the hand is not hindered from approaching the neck with the ball of the little finger; in fact it has the appearance of being half clenched. (See Fig. II).

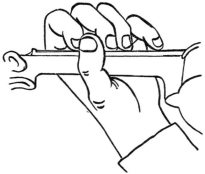

Fig. II. Correct position of the thumb and fingers in the first position, stopping the G-string at a, b, c and d.

After the fourth position is reached, the thumb can not remain longer directly opposite the middle finger, since already in the third position it has touched the point where

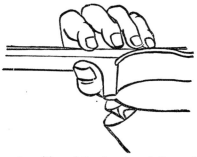

Fig. III. Correct position of the thumb and fingers in the fourth position, stopping the G-string at d, e, f and g.

the neck thickens in anticipation of the block. Beginning with the fourth position then, the thumb remains behind, its lower joint resting against the thick portion of the neck;

thence, in obedience to the demands of comfort as the hand shifts to higher positions, it is gradually withdrawn toward the right until the tip alone remains in contact with the neck. (See Figs. III and IV). Small hands, indeed, are

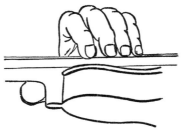

Fig. IV. Correct position of the thumb and and fingers in the seventh position, stopping the G-string at g, a, b and c.

sometimes compelled to withdraw even the tip of the thumb from the neck of the violin; this is unfortunate, as it embarrasses the return of the hand to the earlier positions.

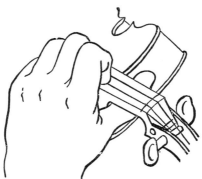

Fig. V. Front view of the correct position of the thumb and fingers in the fourth position, stopping the A-string at e, f, g and ä.

In the fourth position, and, under certain circumstances, in the third, the ball of the thumb touches the body of the violin; it must not rest against it, however, but remain entirely free, the increase in the width and curve of the finger-board augmenting, very materially, the extent of the movements required to control the different strings. After the ball of the thumb has taken a position whence it can guarantee certainty to the movement of the hand, it is no longer necessary to press the base of the forefinger against the neck; on the contrary, this should be forbidden, for to do so would render it difficult to bring the other side of the hand near to the strings, whereas, by relieving the finger of this duty, the knuckle-joints of the four fingers can be kept almost parallel with the strings; and this is essential to the control of high positions on the low strings. Double and triple stopping in the first, second, and third positions are also facilitated, sometimes, by withdrawing the forefinger from the neck.

As the fingers become familiar with the positions on the finger-board, the importance of having fixed places for the thumb decreases. There are, indeed, cases in which the prescriptions become a hindrance; for instance, in the case of a long leap, particularly in legato playing. In such cases, to avoid a stumbling over the third or fourth positions, the tip of the thumb is drawn under the neck at the outset, so that when the shift is made it only will come in contact with the thick portion of the neck.

It is also possible, at times, to find, in accordance with the same principle, a seat of operation for the thumb, whence it can govern two neighboring positions, the first and second, third and fourth; especially from which it can facilitate the change from the second, third, and sometimes fourth, to the first position. In these cases, the shifting of the hand is anticipated by that of the thumb. Aside from the fact that this is a security against disturbing the position of the violin by the movement of the hand, it is in this manner alone that a sure and beautiful portamento can be secured.

To sum up: To the hand of the trained violinist the

thumb performs the functions of a guide, nothing more nor less. It mediates between the fingers and the instrument, inspires their movements with confidence, and aids in securing a firm position to the violin. It should not be underestimated, nor should we presume to call its direct aid—as little as that of the body of the hand—to the purposes of correct intonation.

SECTION IV.

POSITIONS AND ACTION OF THE FINGERS.

It has already been said that the tips of the fingers must stand perpendicularly upon the strings. The following regulations are equally important:

1. All the fingers must hold their first and middle joints bent, when off, as well as when on, the strings; they must move only at the third or knuckle-joints, coming down like a hammer, otherwise the exact spot which they govern on the string can not be found a second time with certainty.

2. The fingers must be lifted from the string with the same precision that they are put down, for many passages, the descending scale for instance, are formed almost wholly by lifting the fingers.

3. After the finger has been lifted it must hover over the point on the string in readiness for a renewal of the application, unless a change of the point is foreseen. That is to say, if the relation of one finger to another on the string was that of a semi-tone, it must retain the same relative position in the air.

4. The fingers must not crowd or brush against each other; this occasions mutual disturbance of position.

5. All unnecessary or irrelevant movements must be carefully avoided; they cause uncertainty and loss of power and time.

It is well to cultivate strength and independence in the fingers by lifting them as high as is consistent with the correct position of the hand, and by applying them to the strings with a sharp, audible blow upon the finger-board. *A finger should never be raised from the string unless it is necessary!* This is an important precept, and here is its complement: *whenever it is possible, the tone should be located on the string, and the finger applied, in advance of the bow.*

These two laws are imperative when two tones upon neighboring strings are to be slurred; the slur can be executed purely and smoothly only by retaining the pressure upon the first string and getting the second ready before the bow touches its string. In all cases obedience to these rules is important, since purity of intonation, dexterity, power, and endurance are very materially furthered by their practice.

Pre-application of the fingers is likewise necessary when a lower finger is hastily called into use after a higher one, as, for instance, in the following examples:

In the first example occurs the need of a pre-application of the second and first fingers; in the second, of the second finger; in the third, of the first, third, and fourth fingers; and in the last, of the first finger.

Investigation will show that in stopping the strings the fingers employ a two-fold action. If a tone is to be retained, an even pressure, lasting till the moment of cessation, is

---

* The lines following the figures indicate the length of time that the finger is to be held upon the string.

requisite. In rapid passages, however, when each finger is concerned only in the instant of application, being relieved immediately after, speed takes the place of power (as used in continuous pressure). That the muscular action in these two functions differs, can be proved by playing these figures:

In the trill both agencies are applied, pressure from the lower, speed from the upper; it is therefore much more difficult to acquire with the little and ring fingers than with the others.

A few additional suggestions are necessary for the promotion of correctness in fingering in the event of changes of position.

1. If a change of position becomes necessary or desirable, after a rest, or after the use of an open string, it must be made independently; that is, there must be no audible slide from the old position to the new. That abominable habit of unpolished vocalists, of prefacing every high note with a deep chest tone and an ascending slide, should not be imitated by violinists.

2. If a lower finger is obliged to pass a higher, the latter must not leave the string until the very moment of the shift, otherwise instead of a pure figure (1) will sound a corrupted one (2):

3. In the reverse case, to avoid a similar corruption, the finger that is to be applied first after the shift must not fall until the hand has arrived at the proper position. (See examples 3 and 4 above.)

4. That which, under the last rule, the majority of beginners do involuntarily, since the first finger shifts the position, must be emphasized as a rule when, in ascending, a higher finger, or, in descending, a lower finger, than the shifting one, is to be used. The hand, supported by the finger last used in the old position, is to be moved until this finger reaches its proper place in the new position ; so that every other finger can take its bearings from it. It is plain that, in ascending, the higher finger must not touch the string, or in descending, leave the string, before the position is reached.

Not thus, but thus: effect. Not thus, but thus: effect.

SECTION V.

INTONATION.

By following the foregoing instructions, a knowledge of the distances upon the strings for all musical intervals and how to reach them with certainty can be acquired with comparative ease and rapidity.

In changing from one string to another, it is well to learn the relation of the tones as effected by a transposition of a fifth (the difference of pitch between the open strings). For instance, the minor sixth on two strings, corresponds with a half step upon one, viz :

Sul D   A   D

The perfect fourth, with a descending whole step:

The major third, with the minor third, and *vice versa:*

Beginners are strongly urged to distinguish sharply between whole and half steps, major and minor, augmented, perfect, and diminished intervals. They are prone to be misled by the customary notation, and the circumstance that upon the violin, for the greater part, the same finger is used for an interval together with its elevation (by a sharp), and its depression (by a flat), to look upon these modifications as homogeneous, and to treat the difference in place upon the string too lightly. The truth is, these modified notes and fingerings are entirely foreign to each other; in fact, the elevation or depression of an interval requires a greater change of position on the string than does the interval of a semi-tone in the diatonic scale.

Consonant intervals can be tested by means of the so-called resultant or difference tones. (See Helmholtz's "Lehre von den Tonempfindungen," third edition, page 242; Tyndall "On Sound," third edition, page 375.) The union of two tones, under certain conditions, produces other tones in the air, which are distinct from the primaries concerned in their production. These tones are, in general, called resultant tones; the most audible one of them is called the difference tone, because of its law, which is, that it corresponds to a rate of vibration equal to the difference of the rates of the two primaries. The difference tones of consonants are always consonant to both tones employed in their production. Consonant intervals produce difference tones according to the following scheme: *

An octave, its own fundamental tone (barely perceptible);

A fifth, the lower octave of its tonic (to be observed in tuning);

A fourth, the second octave below of its upper tone;

A major third, the second octave below of its tonic;

A minor third, the second octave below of the major third;

A major sixth, the fifth below of its fundamental tone;

A minor sixth, the major sixth below of its fundamental tone.

The player should accustom himself to test these intervals by listening for the resultant tones, whenever they come in double stops; if in melodic steps, during practice, he should, if possible, sound them together, or call to his assistance another violin. The following example affords the proper experiments (the resultant tones are designated as quarter notes):

8va lower - - - -

The higher we ascend upon the string, the smaller become the distances that mark the intervals. The explana-

* The following table gives a clearer presentation of the resultant tones:

Interval.	Rate of Vibrations.	Difference.	The resultant tone is deeper than the lowest primary by
Octave	1:2	1	0.
Fifth	2:3	1	An octave.
Fourth	3:4	1	A twelfth.
Major third	4:5	1	Two octaves.
Minor third	5:6	1	Two octaves and a major third.
Major sixth	3:5	2	A fifth.
Minor sixth	5:8	3	A major sixth.

tion of this fact is this: every stop divides the string into two parts, which bear a simple mathematical relationship to each other. The plainest example is the octave. The first octave of an open string is found by stopping, or dividing, it exactly in the middle; the second by dividing the remaining half again in the middle, *i. e.*, stopping the string at the third quarter from the nut; the third by dividing the remaining quarter, leaving one-eighth of the string to vibrate. The chromatic or diatonic contents of an octave, from the open *E*-string to the note on the third line above, are crowded into one-half this distance in the octave from the third line to the seventh space above; so that every finger-space in the higher octave is only one-half as great as in the lower.

The difference of a fifth between the same stop on two neighboring strings remains even along the whole length of the strings, since the nut and bridge fix the same limits for both. This depends, however, upon an equal thickness throughout the entire length of each string, for if the string should taper, the octave would be shifted from the middle. Perfect intonation, therefore, depends upon the use of strings that will tune in perfect fifths.

It may be added that it is not necessary to keep the hand in the same position for all the keys; it is permissible to advance it slightly for the sharp keys and retreat it for the flat keys, but this entails extreme care in shifting.

PART 2.

THE RIGHT SIDE.—TONE PRODUCTION.

SECTION VI.

HOW TO HOLD THE BOW.

A reliable hold upon the bow is a condition precedent for sure and correct manipulation of it. This depends upon obedience to the following precepts:

1. The bow should be held securely; its weight must not draw it from the hand nor disturb its position.

2. The hand should expend as little strength as possible in supporting the bow, so that it may be entirely free to control the nuances of tone.

The wrist should occupy a relation to the bow, so that its most convenient and easy movements can be utilized in changing the stroke from one string to another.

The best hold therefore is the following one:

The thumb should be placed, not against, but within the nut; if the opening in the nut is too narrow because of the grooved projection which slides along the stick, cut away the corners as much as is necessary—they are useless. The nail of the thumb should set against the metal band which receives the hair as it enters the nut, and should never leave this position during the bowing. Certain bowings are impossible unless the thumb-joint be elastic; the thumb, therefore, should not be forced forward as though to resist the pressure of the fingers, nor should it be bent to any consider-able extent. Its best position is the natural one, the one it assumes when in supination. By pinching the thumb against the stick the elasticity of the joint is destroyed, and an ex-cessive bend tends to cramp the ball of the hand; the first fault is produced by thrusting too much of the thumb into the nut, the second, too little.

The four fingers should be laid against the stick opposite the thumb, neither crowded nor spread out, but in an easy and natural position, and so far to the left that both the fore-finger and middle finger will lie forward of the thumb.

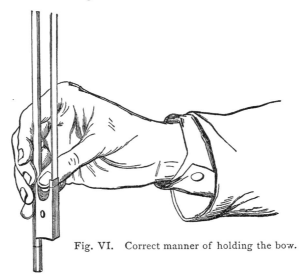

Fig. VI.   Correct manner of holding the bow.

It is a common statement, in books and from teachers, that the bow is held by the thumb, fore-finger and little finger. It is more exact to say: the two outside fingers have a particular function to fulfill, while the inside (middle and ring) fingers aid the thumb in holding the bow; this is done principally by the middle finger, which, by bending its first joint around the stick prevents it from slipping from the grasp. Each player must determine for himself how far the finger can extend over the stick, whether to the joint or not, but care must be taken that it does not extend so far that, in bowing near the nut, the tip of the finger comes in contact with the strings. The ring-finger, however, must not reach so far, because, it being shorter, to lay the bend of its first joint across the stick, would compel a turn of the hand toward the lower end of the bow.

The little finger is called upon to resist the weight of the bow, to prevent the upper end from overbalancing the lower during the stroke and to lift it entirely free from the strings. The center of gravity being, generally, at one-third the length of the bow from the nut, the little finger becomes superfluous so soon as the middle or upper part of the bow rests upon the string; it is well, however, to permit it always to remain in contact with the stick, since its feeling will at once detect a change in the position of the hand. It should be extended and rest with its tip full upon the stick, so that it will not slip off on either side. Heavy bows, or large bows in small hands, necessitate that the little finger should be parted more widely from the others than is usually the case, in order that it may better resist the weight of the bow; but this is calculated to hamper the freedom of the wrist-joint.

The particular function of the fore-finger is to exert the needed pressure upon the bow for the purpose of accentuation and to swell the power of the tone. This pressure must be elastic, and to this end the finger must not be charged with any other duty, but must lie upon the stick with all joints supine, the second joint, not the bend, crossing the stick. It is unnecessary, and consequently inadvisable, to press the tip against the stick; it would be a waste of strength, and worse than that, it might divert the pressure of the bow upon he strings from a perpendicular to an oblique one toward the bridge of the violin.

The first joints of the middle and ring fingers should also be held supine, so as to entail no exertion on the muscles of the hand. The pressure of the little finger is the only effort required to hold and carry the bow.

If the fingers are applied to the bow as has been described, they will be at almost right angles to it, their bases being a trifle behind their tips. The thumb, however, with its base under that of the fore-finger, and its tip between the tips of the middle and ring fingers, can not describe a right angle, with the bow, but instead slants from its base toward the tip of the ring-finger. The circumstance, too, that the fingers lie flat upon the stick compels the thumb to come in contact with the nut near its sides instead of with its full front and nail. The flesh will touch the stick near the inner side of the thumb, the nail will touch the metal ring of the nut with its outer edge. The relative position of the thumb towards the fingers is such that it can not be brought directly in front of any of them, and consequently if it were placed full against the bow, it would tilt the hand to the left. (See Fig. VII.)

Fig. VII. Showing the relative positions of the thumb and fingers.

If the bow be now grasped in the manner prescribed, and held horizontally, it will be seen that the knuckles of the hand are almost on a line ; the base of the fore-finger will be no lower than the bases of the ring and little fingers, but the base of the middle finger will be somewhat higher. Consequently the back of the hand does not slant downwards toward the left, nor is the wrist turned; *the axis of the wrist-joint runs parallel with the bow.* (See Figs. VIII and IX.)

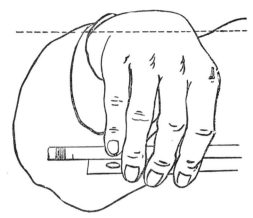

Fig. VIII.   Correct position of the hand and wrist, showing the parallel between the axis of the joint and the bow.

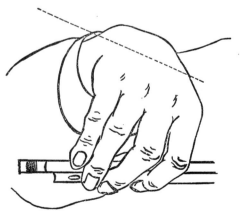

Fig. IX.   Incorrect position of the wrist, the hand tilted downward toward the left.

The movement around this axis is the simplest possible action of the wrist–joint, and the fact that it can serve to carry the bow from one string to its neighbor (it being at right angles with the direction of the moving bow), is proof of the superiority and efficiency of the hold which has been described. In view of this function of the wrist–joint, a caution must be pronounced against a constrained, or convulsive, clutching of the bow.

The majority of violinists tilt the hand in the direction of the fore-finger. This prevents the use of the simplest movement of which the wrist-joint is capable; the movement will become either a twist, or the transfer of the bow from one string to the other will be accomplished by the action of the elbow or shoulder, because the bend of the joint around its axis under these circumstances would push the bow sidewise. Sometimes even the moving bow is met by a turn of the violin, accompanied by a motion of the entire left side of the body, and the uncertainty is aggravated by unrest. In all respects, but especially in this, correct and certain bowing can only be acquired if the violin is held in a uniform and hence immovable position.

SECTION VII.

POSITION OF THE BOW ON THE STRINGS. PRESERVATION OF ITS DIRECTION. EQUALITY OF TONE.

Clearness and equality of tone, especially in very soft playing, are conditioned upon obedience to these precepts, viz:

1. The string must be excited to *lateral* vibrations; or, in other words, *the bow must cross the strings at right angles.*

2. The vibrations must be sent out from the smallest possible point of contact, *i. e.*, the whole surface of the hair must not brush the string, but only the edge.

3. The bow should not, unless for a special purpose, change the location of the point of contact with the strings; it must not be jostled or shoved to one side while sounding a tone.

Careful investigation and study is necessary concerning the method to be employed in keeping the bow at right angles to the strings throughout the stroke, since, on this point, many incorrect expressions are current. Louis Spohr, for instance, in his great "Violin School," and after him, Ferdinand David, teaches, strangely enough, that the straight course of the bow is to be maintained by changing the position of the hand. What prompted this error was doubtless the circumstance that all violinists who have attained independence, are accustomed to round off their changes in bowing, by yielding with all the joints of their fingers and hand; but they never change their grasp of the bow. The result has been a confusion of terms which could never have occurred had these authors been practically engaged in teaching beginners.

The first, and most important, principle in bowing (in direct conflict with this doctrine of Spohr and David,) is that the hand shall, in effect, be one with the bow, *and entirely independent of the arm.* The hand and the bow must describe a straight line through the air at every stroke, and the arm must subordinate itself completely to this requirement, just as the left arm is subordinate to the fingers. By calling in the aid of the eyes, a correct style of bowing can be acquired in the space of a few days. To this end the player should take a position in front of a large mirror (if possible a pier glass); he should stand with his right side toward it, and at such an angle that only the edge of the bridge will be visible in the reflection. If the violin is correctly held, *i. e.,* so high that the strings lie horizontally, the course of the bow will appear, in the reflection, straight up and down.

And now, what will be seen in the glass ?

First, and foremost, if it remains one with the bow, though yielding with all its joints, the hand will not deviate from its position at right angles to the bow.

When the fore-arm extends horizontally, the hand will be found to be in a line with it. This occurs when the bow touches the strings above its middle, say at its upper one-third. The use of the upper third, therefore, requires a bending of the hand to the right. (See Fig. X.)

This applies to an arm of medium length ; a very long arm reaches lower, so that the point at which the fore-arm and hand are in a line, is nearer the point of the bow; hence a smaller bend of the hand is required to reach it. When the arm is very small, the point at which the fore-arm becomes horizontal is not far from the middle of the stroke, and a large and even painful bend of the hand is required to reach the point. Relief from this must be sought in the privilege described hereafter.

If it becomes necessary to lower the wrist-joint so much that the entire surface of the hair touches the strings, or that the contact is changed from the outer to the inner edge, or that the bow is drawn from its proper course inwardly, it is evidence that *the bow is too long.* In such cases it is best to modify the requirement that the bow be drawn to its point, and to designate, by a chalk-mark upon the stick, the point that is to serve instead as the end of the stroke. Beginners are often inclined to try to reach the point of the bow by relaxing their hold (withdrawing the little-finger and changing the position of the fore-finger); for this reason it is well to place the limitation of the stroke, at first, within easy reach.

And now as to the relative positions of the elbow and shoulder.

When the bow is applied to the strings at its point and at right angles, the upper part of the arm (which is properly

Fig. X. Variations in the position of the right arm in executing a stroke; *a*, at the point of the bow; *b*, in the middle; *c*, at the nut. The extremes of the bow are indicated by corresponding letters. The left hand is in the first position, the fingers stopping the *E*-string at *f*, *g*, *a*, *b*.

called the arm in contradistinction to the lower part, called the fore-arm, and which will hereafter be so designated,) will not hang perpendicularly, but will be forward of the shoulder. An upward motion of the fore-arm begins the stroke, which can be continued until the horizontal position is slightly passed, without threatening to push the bow over the bridge; the moment that this danger seems imminent, however, this motion of the fore-arm must cease. This stroke of the fore-arm, executed by movement from the elbow-joint is coincident, in the case of small arms, to the use of the upper half of the bow; long arms control somewhat less. It is important to note that in this stroke, the hand is bent sidewise in both directions as the horizontal line is passed on both sides by the fore-arm.

When the fore-arm can go no further without disturbing the direction of the bow, there begins a forward movement of the arm, which pushes the fore-arm and hand until the nut of the bow reaches the strings.

Beginners should first study the fore-arm stroke (carefully noting the point of change), then the arm stroke, and then the two united; a short pause should at first be made at the dividing point, and then the stroke should be practiced with a continuous movement. The purpose of this is to prevent the impression that the stroke is a *mixed* action of the elbow and shoulder joints. By mixing the actions of these joints the bow would be directed in a serpentine path. In executing a stroke on one string, the relation of the arm toward the body should remain unchanged while the bow moves from point to nut. This is the natural and common-sense rule concerning the raising of the arm sidewise from the body; to change its position, unless through the need caused by a transfer of the bow to another string, would be worse than idle, and would render an already complex action still more complicated. If the arm is raised sufficiently high to enable the point of the bow to be applied to the *G*-string, it is not necessary to depress the elbow in order to reach the string with the nut, but only to push it forward in the line of the fore-arm.

The majority of violin methods lay down the rule that the proper position of the elbow at all times is as near the body as is possible. This is another of those superficial precepts which need only to be analysed to show their absurdity. The plain inference of it is, that if a stroke upon the *G*-string compels a raising of the arm, it should be lowered again as soon as possible, as though strokes upon the low strings were exceptions to the rules of bowing, which are based on the use of the high strings. In this sense there can be no normal position for the arm, but instead *one for each string, and three for strokes on two strings simultaneously, i. e., for double stops.* If the distance of the arm from the body is maintained as we have taught, *the elbow will always remain lower than the hand* after the up-stroke has carried the hand beyond the point where it is in a line with the fore-arm; this is an essential thing, for to raise the elbow higher than the hand disturbs the even pressure of the bow upon the strings, and is a grievous fault. In bowing on the *G*-string, the arm should be depressed about 20° below a line drawn across and and extending beyond the shoulders.

The second direction, given at the beginning of this section, viz: that for very soft tones the edge of the hair only should touch the strings, can best be followed by tipping the bow forward, or toward the finger-board. This places the hand in a position which is less dependent upon the arm than if the full surface of the hair rested upon the strings; at the extremity of the up-stroke, it will be seen that the wrist is not only bent to the left but is slightly raised. In this position of the hand, it will be found impossible, to all except very long arms, to draw the bow to its point; however, the necessity of so long a pianissimo stroke will seldom occur. It is, therefore, unnecessary, besides being uncomfortable, and for these reasons the player need not carry his hand hanging thus in his wrist-joint to the end of the stroke; moreover, it will be found that in passages of medium power this position of the hand would leave him without power to continue the pressure of the bow at the point, which is required for an even sustentation of the tone. Instead, therefore, of holding the bow tipped at the same angle throughout the stroke, he should lessen it as he approaches the point, so that when he reaches it, the hand, if his arm is long, will be on a level with the fore-arm ; if short, with the wrist slightly depressed. The louder the tone that is desired, the greater the freedom that can be taken in this respect, since the pressure itself causes all the hair to touch the strings near the nut, or at least in the middle of the bow. It would be incautious, however, to apply the entire surface of the hair near the nut in playing *forte*, unless a hard and dry quality of tone is desired.

We must here call attention to another current but false impression, viz: that it is by raising and lowering the wrist (which the discussion just had has taught us is to be tolerated, for a different purpose, rather than commanded), that the bow is to be directed in its proper course. If the bow is held improperly, with the hand sloping toward the left, this view is not entirely wrong, but it is confusing if the bow be properly held.

The normal hold and movement is pleasing to the eye ; the player should therefore avoid deviating from it in a mistaken effort to acquire elegance in these respects.

We have already seen that it is more difficult to exert a pressure upon the strings with the point of the bow than with the nut. This is accounted for, not only by the fact that the center of gravity of the bow is below the middle, but also by the fact that it requires a greater expenditure of power to transfer the downward pressure to the strings a distance from the hand than it does to exert it directly on a point immediately below the hand.   Now, for a very natural reason, the weight of the bow being left to operate on the pressure, the tone decreases during a down-stroke, and increases during an up-stroke.   In order, therefore, to preserve equality of tone throughout the stroke, a gradually increasing pressure must be applied from the beginning to the end of a down-stroke, to off-set the gradual loss of weight-pressure ; in an up-bow the operation must, of course, be reversed.   If less pressure is desired than that exerted by the weight of the bow alone, it can be modified to a mere brushing of the strings at the nut by slightly raising the hand and pressing the little finger against the stick.

An effort to execute an extremely light stroke by this means, or to bow through the air just above the strings, will betray, unmistakably, one faulty tendency in bowing, viz: to execute the down-stroke by dropping the arm, and the up-stroke by raising it.

The action of the muscles, not the weight of the arm, must influence the stroke.

The point of contact upon the strings is not a fixed one.   In playing upon the open strings and a few of the lower stopped—tones, it is best to apply the bow mid-way between the bridge and finger-board, just above the forward end of the *F*-holes ; in high positions or *forte* playing the bow involuntarily approaches the bridge ; in *pianissimo* passages play nearer the finger-board.   On thin strings the bridge can be approached closer than on thick.

SECTION VIII.

DIVISIONS OF THE STROKE.

From the fact that a uniformly rapid stroke (with the co-operation of a properly regulated pressure, as has just been described,) must correspond with a uniform tone-power, the rule is deduced that several strokes of equal duration require equal lengths of bow if equality of tone-power is desired; while strokes of irregular duration must be so conditioned that their lengths can be divided to conform to their duration.

Take, for instance, a quiet hymn-tune, composed of whole, half, and quarter notes, which are not separated by rests nor tied. Here the whole notes will receive the whole bow, the half notes half of the bow, and the quarter notes one-quarter of the bow. This need grows out of the simple fact that rapidity of stroke, as well as increase of pressure, excite the strings to more violent vibrations and hence louder tones.

This division is repeated again in examples on a smaller scale, for instance, in passages from Allegro movements, when the notes are of irregular duration, or, if regular, partly slurred, partly detached,—and can, indeed, be sub-divided until single notes between ties are played by a movement of the hand alone instead of the arm. (See "Wrist-Stroke.")

When sharp accentuation is desired, in cases of this character, it is desirable that the short stroke should be executed with the down-bow; for this reason it has become customary in orchestras to play syncopated notes with the down-bow, even if the preceding stroke was the same.

When the bowing threatens to become embarrassingly inconvenient, the corrective consists in a second application

of the bow in the same direction ; which is done in three
ways, viz :

1. By breaking off the stroke and returning to the
beginning.

2. By stopping and starting again from the point reached.

3. By momentarily lifting the bow from the strings
while continuing the stroke.

This latter method is very difficult, but is productive of
beautiful effects in appropriate cantabiles.

The habit of reading the bowing at a glance from the
notes and the facility of promptly applying the proper
corrective in case of necessity, should be cultivated in the
beginner by carefully marking the music and closely following
the directions.

SECTION IX.

GRADUATION OF TONE-POWER. [NUANCES.]

The most potent medium of musical expression lies in
dynamic variation. The importance of the subject of nuances
is evident from the fact that a sustained tone, which neither
increases nor decreases in power, creates the impression of
lifelessness, of monotony, and indifference. Every person
gifted in any degree with a musical faculty perceives at once
that the correctness of a series of tones with regard to their
pitch and duration, is not a sufficient power to move a listener.

The question of tone graduation, however, includes more
than the increasing and decreasing of the volume of sound ;
it includes accentuation, which is an ever-present requirement,
whether marked by the composer or not, because it publishes
the *rhythm* to the listener. In this respect the good old law
is peculiarly apt, despite all modern tendencies : when the
contrary is not prescribed the thesis must be accented, the
arsis treated lighter. This accent should not be exaggerated,

else it will appear to the listener, not as an effort to mark the rhythm for his benefit, but as a *pons asinorum* which the player uses to keep himself advised of the rhythmical movement of the music. Unfortunately, one abuse of this kind is very wide-spread, viz: the practice of accenting the thesis in syncopated passages by increasing the pressure of the bow upon the strings. This is directly contrary to the nature of a syncopation, which seeks its effects in irregular accentuation, and is a marked exception to the rule. Singers and performers on wind instruments and the piano never think of doing this—a pianist, indeed, can not—how comes it, then, to be so common a fault with violinists?

It is hardly necessary to refer to the manipulation required to swell the tone; it is done by increasing the pressure of the bow or the speed of the stroke, or both. For the usual accent a pressure suffices; for very marked accents a jerk in the stroke can assist. In all cases when a particular effect is sought to be attained by a crescendo during a stroke or a series of long strokes, increase in pressure must be supplemented by increase in speed, and *vice versa*.

The same principle is likewise applicable to the division of the bow in passages of variable power, so that in a sustained, singing melody, an accented quarter-note may require the whole bow, while a soft half-note will require only half the length. How comical an embarrassment can be prepared by inadvertence in this regard, can be illustrated by a notorious instance. A great many musicians have the habit, and a very commendable one it is, of using as many whole-bows as possible, for the sake of the smoothness and gracefulness of the flow of tone which the practice promotes. But, suppose, an eighth-note falls upon the up-beat, and is followed immediately by a stroke comprehending a whole measure of 4-4 time, dare we then give the whole length of the bow to the up-beat? The practice is almost universal, and yet the right of the thesis in the second measure to accent, should induce caution against the waste of power on the up-beat.

For variations of power in passages there is no trustworthy means, except obedience to this rule: treat *forte* with long, and *piano* with short strokes, particularly when playing in the orchestra. For the latter use of the bow the French have the term "demi-jeu"—half-play.

The mechanics for increasing and decreasing the tone should be much and carefully studied, for it is very difficult to acquire the knack of doing this smoothly and gradually. As is manifest from what was said on a previous page concerning the weight of the bow, the *crescendo* is most easily executed with the up-stroke, the *diminuendo*, with the down.

SECTION X.

BOWING.

As distinguished from those divisions of the bow which related to irregular durations, irregular lengths, and irregular tone-power, we have now to discuss methods of bowing for regular successions of tones of equal duration and power.

The first thing to be noted in a passage of this character is: whether it is slow enough to admit of the use of the whole bow; if not, fractions of the bow will suffice. Secondly, the style of the succession is to be considered: are the notes to be slurred or detached? We therefore distinguish between

1. WHOLE BOWS WITH SLURRED TONES; and
2. WHOLE BOWS WITH DETACHED TONES.

The first style was suggested in Sec. VII in the phrase: "to round off their changes in bowing," and it was there remarked that this effect was to be obtained by yielding with all the joints of the hand, but not by a change of its position toward the bow. It is the flexibility of the first thumb-joint that makes possible a change of the stroke in this manner. Excessive flexibility, however, results in producing a nervous jerk of the tone at each change of the stroke, particularly at the nut end of the bow—a fault which is too often taught, instead of being condemned. By carefully avoiding this exaggerated style, it is possible to change the stroke either at the end or any other portion of the bow so imperceptibly that the aid of the eye is required for its detection.

The opposite of this is the marked or sharp attack of each note. For this the bow should be applied to the string and pressed sharply against it an instant before the tone is desired, so that it will sound promptly and decisively the moment the bow is moved; after the bow begins to move, however, the pressure should be continued only in case the stroke is a quiet, long-drawn one ; if a vehement one, the initial pressure is sufficient, and must be modified *at once.*

What fractions of the bow can be used in bowing? First, as to the province of the fore-arm, where we distinguish, as before, between

    3. SLURRED ; and

    4. DETACHED, FORE-ARM STROKE.

Nothing need be added to what has been said concerning the former style; but some remarks are needed concerning the latter, which, when given forcibly, is called *martellato,* or *martelé.* It is best not to use the whole territory of the fore-arm for this stroke, when it controls the entire upper half of the bow, for the reason that a sharp attack with the surface of the hair sounds badly on the down-stroke ; the attack should be made with the edge of the hair. The precept that was announced for the vehement whole bow-stroke, viz.: That the pressure of the bow must be instantly modified, is specially applicable here. To stop the bow while maintaining the pressure smothers the tone ; whereas, for the very reason that the bow ceases to operate so quickly, the string should be permitted to vibrate. Here, too, another difficulty comes to the front, which is less palpable in detached strokes of the whole bow. In these, as well as in fore-arm strokes, care must be had that the strokes are made sufficiently short to separate the notes, and gain time for the new attack; in the fore-arm stroke, however, the player is peculiarly liable to uncertainty as to how great a distance he can move from the point (in the up-stroke), and this, together with the difficulty of an attack from the point, tends to produce a faulty stroke. The player should therefore note carefully with the eye and feeling how large a section of the bow he is using.

In rapid tempos, or for less tone-power, a smaller fraction of the bow, *but always near the point*, is to be used. It is possible to use an incisive attack even in the softest pianissimo ; then, however, the movement of the fore-arm is hardly perceptible.

The action of the hand in exerting the pressure for the attack, may, and indeed should, be perceptible, as also the approach of the stick to the hair which it causes.

A repetition of these detached tones in the same stroke is called *staccato*. A few staccato strokes occurring in moderate tempo can be executed in any part of the bow without difficulty. In more extended and rapid passages, the sharply defined attack becomes impossible ; there is, instead, a shoving movement of the hand which can be perfectly regulated, as to the number of strokes, by practice, especially if the rule is followed of slightly accenting the first and last strokes, which generally fall upon the accented parts of the measure. The best effects in rapid staccato playing are secured by the use of the up-stroke and the upper half of the bow.

For very rapid passages, particularly when played *piano*,

even the fore-arm stroke is too clumsy; in such cases we make use of

5. THE WRIST-STROKE.

The action of the hand in this stroke must be carefully distinguished from that which transfers the bow from string to string. The movement is a lateral swing of the hand, and is hardly possible without a slight tilt of the hand towards the fore-finger, and sometimes a lifting of the little finger from the stick. The movement can be executed with any part of the bow, but it is most sure at the nut end, in which case, however, the service of the little finger can not be spared. The whole arm should be held perfectly quiet, the thumb-joint entirely relaxed, and the bow be moved quietly across the string by a swinging motion of the hand. There should be no effort to make the stroke as long as is possible; on the contrary it should be as short as the natural, unconstrained movement makes it.

If the point of contact be now changed from the end to the middle of the bow, it will be seen that every stroke sways the stick up and down, and if the force of the stroke be increased, the hair will leap from the strings. This *springing bow* is the means of producing one of the most fascinating effects obtainable from the violin. If it is not desired, the point of contact must be shifted somewhat and the action of the hand modified.

The wrist-stroke can be cultivated to such a degree of rapidity that it is impossible to count the strokes given in a measure. This exceedingly rapid division of a note is called *tremolo*.

Naturally the wrist-stroke is most powerful at the nut, as is also the thrown stroke to be discussed further on. The greater the distance from the nut at which these strokes are used, the smaller the tone-power. This is to be remembered in connection with the study of nuances.

For passages that are not too rapid, and which require a good volume of tone, a combination of the fore-arm and wrist-strokes can be used, that is, a fore-arm stroke extended at both extremities by a swing of the hand, or, if the definition be preferred, a wrist-stroke augmented by a movement of the fore-arm. It is much less wearisome than the fore-arm stroke of equal rapidity.

If the springing bow is desired in a passage of slow tempo, it can be had through the use of

6. THE THROWN STROKE.

This stroke can be executed at the nut, or with the lower third of the bow by a movement of the arm, or near the middle by a movement of the fore-arm. When very near the nut it becomes so hard and dry that it might be called the *chopping stroke*. In this stroke, as in the last, the wrist-joint is to be kept perfectly loose. As the middle of the bow is neared, the action of the wrist becomes freer and the movement of the arm correspondingly less in extent and greater in rapidity, and then the change from the thrown stroke to the springing bow can easily be made. Above the middle of the bow the stroke becomes exaggerated to a lashing of the strings, producing an effect which, like the chopping stroke, is very limited in its application.

Like the detached stroke, the thrown stroke can be repeated a number of times in the same direction, either (and this without difficulty, when the arm is used,) by a reapplication of the same part of the bow, where there is sufficient time between the notes to recover (Example 1); then (especially in an up-stroke), without recovering the bow when the thrown strokes are few in number (Example 2); it is also possible to connect a broad stroke with a short thrown one (Example 3).

Compare section VIII, page 37, on the first and second methods of dividing the stroke. In connection with the third method, which is applicable here, since broad strokes are in question, the following is an example of a style which was much used by Louis Spohr:

Above the middle of the bow a series of blows can be given in an up-stroke, which are equivalent to a *flying staccato*, that is, a staccato in which the tones are separated by the bow leaping from the strings instead of stopping. Moreover the bow can be permitted, after falling upon the string, to rebound upon it several times, without aid from the hand, which must, of course, be held very loosely. For this the downstroke and upper half of the bow should be used. The effect is exceedingly graceful and arch, and especially useful in humorous music.

In one view of the matter, that division of the stroke which best meets the demands of a continued dotted rhythm, viz: a continuation in the same direction for the short note after the dot, can also be looked upon as a method of bowing. In a rapid tempo the listener conceives the short note as rhythmically connected with the succeeding, not the preceding, dotted note; he hears it as an up-beat, for which reason it is proper to use rests instead of dots in rapid movements. The feeling should catch up this thythm in the same way; *the stroke is changed on the long note, and every long note is preceded by a preparatory short stroke in the former direction.*

Naturally, too, the long note receives an accentuation, and, owing to its time-value and rhythmical position, a greater length of the bow; the short note, accordingly, is often produced by a mere swing of the hand, while the long one receives the action of the fore-arm. In an extremely rapid tempo it is seldom possible to give the preparatory stroke in the same direction as the long note preceding, even though the latter be cut off short; resort must then be had to a change on each note with this provision : the long, accented notes are to be given near the point, and with the up-bow ; and this compels great care that the down-bow may be lighter than the up-bow, because the accent falls upon the latter.

The natural tendency being to make the down-strokes more powerful than the up-strokes, it is advisable to study these bowings, when equality of tone is difficult to maintain, in passages of triplets, because then the accents will fall alternately in both strokes ; it is also well, occasionally to reverse the usual process, and begin figures in common time with an up-bow for the purpose of testing the equality of the tone.

SECTION XI.

TECHNICS OF THE WRIST FOR CHANGING THE BOW ON THE STRINGS.

In Section V it was shown that, with the proper hold upon the bow, it is the simplest movement of the wrist-joint—that around its axis—that carries the bow from one string to another. This general proposition is now supplemented with the following particular instructions:

1. The down-bend changes the bow from a lower to a higher, the up-bend from a higher to a lower, string. Beginners are prone to confound these motions.

2. The arm should take a position with relation to the lower of two strings, if they are to be repeatedly exchanged, so that the down-bend toward the higher of the strings will tip the bow forward; if the position were chosen for the arm to accommodate the higher string (that is the one nearest the hand), the up-bend for the change would bring the full surface of the hair upon the string, and this would jeopardize the prompt response of this *thicker* string.

3. At the nut the bend of the hand is so slight that, if the desired change is to the next string, a simple pressure from the little finger can be substituted for it. The greater the distance of the nut from the strings, the greater will be the bend of the hand, and for this reason it should be practiced principally with the point of the bow.

4. If necessary, a transfer to the distance of three strings can be made by the use of the bend of the hand alone; for four strings, however, the assistance of the arm is requisite.

5. If a whole or fore-arm stroke is to be executed on one string, and immediately afterward repeated on a neighboring string, smoothness in the change can be promoted by having the bend of the hand precede the change in the position of the arm.

6. The action of the hand must not be gradual, but prompt and precise; attention can be compelled to this in study by not separating the strokes, but drawing them out to the full value of the note. A too sudden movement, however, might result in disturbing the position of the bow; here, as in all good things, the pursuit of the goldèn mean is the wisest course.

The practice of these wrist movements should be taken up by beginners so soon as the fore-arm stroke is learned; at first little of the bow should be used, and the stroke should be very light, so that the purpose of the proceeding may become perfectly plain. A great many beginners are guilty of trying to squeeze the bow from one string to its neighbor, thereby exerting themselves unnecessarily, and stiffening their wrist-joints to the injury of the correct motion.

APPENDIX.

A LIST OF VALUABLE WORKS OF INSTRUCTION
FOR THE VIOLIN.

BACH, J. S. 6 Celebrated Violin Sonatas. New edition, revised by
Edouard Herrmann.

BÉRIOT, CHAS. DE. Violin Method. Part I. New edition, revised
and annotated by G. Lehmann.

— Op. 17. 6 Études brillantes. Preparatory to Op. 20 and 39.
Material for the cultivation of brilliancy.

DANCLA, CH. Duos Concertants. Op. 23, 32, 60, 24, 33.
Progressive Duets in the first position. Excellent for sight
reading.

— Duos Concertants. Op. 61, 15, 34, 62, 25, 35.
These seldom exceed 4th position.

— Duos Concertants. Op. 43, 63, 64.
Extend to the higher positions.

— Op. 74. École de Mécanisme. 50 Exercises.
These short exercises are well adapted to improve the technic of
the fingers in the different positions.

DAVID, FERD. "Concert Studien":

1. Viotti, J. B. Concertos—Nos. 23, 28, 29, 22.
2. Rode, P. Concertos—Nos. 4, 6, 7, 8.
3. Kreutzer, R. Concertos—Nos. 13, 14, 18, 19.

DONT, J. Op. 37. 24 Preparatory Studies to Kreutzer and Rode's
exercises.

— Op. 38. 20 Exercises (with a Second Violin).

FIORILLO, F. 36 Caprices (revised by Schradieck).
These are as indispensable as Kreutzer's in the development of
the technical as well as the artistical part of Violin-playing.

GAVINIÉS, P. 24 Études.
Very important for the final development of the left hand.

GRUENBERG, EUGENE. The Violinist's Manual.

> A progressive classification of technical material, études, solo pieces, and the most important chamber-music works, as well as a short synopsis of the literature of the Viola, to which is added hints for the Violinist.

HERING, C. Op. 13. Elementary Violin School.

> Very practical.

— Op. 20. 10 Studies, in the first position.

> These prepare for the Kreutzer Studies.

— Op. 16. The Major and Minor Scales. 25 Exercises (with a Second Violin).

> Excellent in developing the technic of the fingers and the bow.

— Op. 37. Bluethenkrärze, and Op. 61, Erstlingssprossen. A collection of songs in the first position, with piano or Second Violin.

HAUSER, M. 12 Études de Concert. Part I, Op. 8; Part II, Op. 33.

> Useful for acquiring ease of execution; to be played prior to David's Op. 20 and 39.

HOHMANN, C. H. Practical Method for Violin. New and enlarged edition by Ph. Mittell.

> A standard work, known throughout the world.

KAYSER, H. E. Op. 37. Parts I, II, III. "The first Teacher of Violin-playing."

— Op. 37. Parts IV, V, VI. Daily Exercises preparatory to his Op. 20.

— Op. 20. 36 Progressive Studies.

> Very useful as preparatory studies to Kreutzer.

— Op. 44. 50 Short Exercises. Part I in the first position.

— Op. 40. 32 Light Pieces in the first position, with a Second Violin.

KREUTZER, R. 42 Studies (revised by E. Singer).

> These classical studies are indispensable to every Violin-player who aims at the true art of Violin-playing.

LANGHANS, W. Op. 5. 20 Études. First position.

LEHMANN, GEORGE. The True Principles of Violin-playing.

> The author, well knowing that students not only waste much valuable time by following faulty methods, but are often prevented thereby from reaching full artistic development, offers in this little work the practical fruits of a serious study of the fundamental principles underlying violin-technics.

LEONARD, H.   Op. 21.   24 Études Classiques.
>   Pleasing, and admirable in developing the artistic faculty.

MAZAS, F.   Op. 36.   Vols. I, II, III.   75 Melodious and Progressive Studies.
>   Very useful.

MEERTS, L. J.   The Mechanism of the Bow.   12 Études.
>   Very practical in developing firm bowing.

PAGANINI.   24 Caprices.
>   These caprices are regarded as being the most difficult written, and are celebrated for their cultivation of the highest accomplishments in the line of bravura-playing.

PRUME, F.   Op. 14.   6 Études de Concert.
>   For the development of bravura-playing.

RIES, HUBERT.   Violin School.   Parts I and II.

— Op. 28.   30 Elementary Studies.

RODE, P.   Op. 22.   24 Caprices.   Revised by David.
>   These classical studies are, with Kreutzer's and Fiorillo's, the most important in our violin literature, and tend to develop the musical and higher artistic style of violin-playing.

SCHRADIECK, H.   The First Position.   The Elements of Violin-playing.

— Technical Violin School.   New edition, revised and enlarged by the author.   Part I—Exercises to increase certainty in the different positions.   Part II—Exercises in double stopping. Part III—Exercises in the different modes of bowing.

— Scale Studies.   New edition, revised by the author.
>   There is nothing in all violin literature which replaces these scales in clearness of purpose and practicability.

SCHUBERT, L.   Op. 50.   Violin Method.

SINGER, ED.   Daily Finger Exercises.
>   Excellent for strengthening the fingers.

TARTINI, J.   L'Art de l'Archet.   50 Variations.
>   A renowned and very important work for the artistic development of bowing, and of the left hand.

WILHELMJ, A.   A School of Thirds.
>   A most important contribution to the list of technical works for the violin, by one of its greatest masters, consisting of exercises exclusively in thirds, progressively arranged.